Foreword

Most of us, most of the time, live as though the planet is ours for the taking. While humans make up less than one percent of all life on Earth, our activities have helped destroy most wild animals and half of plants on the planet.

As climate change and other 21st century threats cause marine and terrestrial wildlife to abandon habitat and search for new homes, perhaps the most pressing question facing our planet is: are we humans willing to share it? Biodiversity is essential for human society to function, from agriculture and medicine, to clean water and reliable weather. In this light, sharing isn't caring. It's an act of survival.

Confronted with such leviathan challenges we sometimes lose hope, forgetting that small acts and smart daily decisions can have an extraordinary impact on how people and animals can thrive together. E.O. Wilson, perhaps the most venerated biologist of our time, has called for devoting half of the planet's surface to wildlife and wilderness.

How will we get there from here? We don't have to start big; we can start in our own back yards, on our beaches and up and down the coastline along which North Atlantic right whales like Kleenex have migrated for millennia.

Numbering in the tens of thousands before Yankee whalers deemed them the "right" whale to hunt, fewer than 420 of these slow-moving surface swimmers remain today. They face more threats than ever, including lethal entanglement in outmoded fishing gear and deadly collisions with ships. IFAW and our committed partners are racing to the rescue, releasing entangled right whales, helping mariners safely navigate around them, engaging fishermen and other stakeholders in encouraging action by government officials to secure the survival of this critically endangered species.

Beyond supporting these efforts, there are countless decisions each of us can make every day to demonstrate our willingness to share the planet—from the kinds of products we buy, the vacations we take, the careers we pursue, and the causes to which we donate and volunteer our time.

The book you are holding in your hands and the young people of the fifth grade class of P.S. 107 who created it remind us it is not too late. We can move from consumption to contentment, from exploitation to stewardship of right whales and other species. Fresh thinking and bold action today can build a better tomorrow for animals, people, and the planet we call home.

Azzedine T. Downes
President and CEO, International Fund for Animal Welfare

Hello there, humans! My name is Kleenex and this is my story.

NOAA Permit #594-1759

I'm a North Atlantic right whale and a mama to many.

I'm also a grandma and a great grandma. So I am an amazing, strong female whale.

If you want to know how I got my name, it's because I have a white spot on my head, so it looks like there is a tissue by my nose.

Right now I'm about 42 years old, but I think I'm still looking great.

We right whales grow up to be around 50 feet. That's like a school bus and a half. We can weigh up to 140,000 pounds, or 70 tons. Think about swimming being that heavy!

Even though we live in the sea, we're
not fish. We're mammals--just like you.

Mama whales stay with their calves for over a year, nursing and taking care of them.

Before my baby leaves, we take long swims together. It's hard to know that my child will leave.

One fascinating thing about right whales is our way of communicating. We use many types of calls that help us talk and find each other, and to know if any of us are in danger.

I can talk to my family and friends by saying a "whoop."

These sounds can be unique for each whale. It's like humans who each have a unique voice.

We eat copepods for breakfast, lunch, and dinner.

Oh, you don't know what copepods are? Well, they are only the most delicious food in the world! They are tiny shrimp-like creatures, smaller than the nail on your pinky. So to survive, we have to eat a lot of them.

My baleen plates help me catch copepods. Baleen is made up of many thin eight-foot-long bristles in our mouths, like a giant hairbrush.

NOAA Permit # 15488

We catch the copepods by leaving our mouths open while swimming. Once we get enough stuff in our mouths, we filter out the water by pushing it against our baleen plates with our tongues. It filters out all the water, like a sieve. Once all that's left is copepods, we feast.

Every year, my fellow whales and I migrate all along the east coast of North America. In summer, we swim up to Canada, around the Bay of Fundy and the Gulf of Saint Lawrence. Then in winter, we migrate south to the warmer water in Georgia and Florida, where we have our babies.

The journey is almost 2,000 miles.

NOAA permit #15488

14

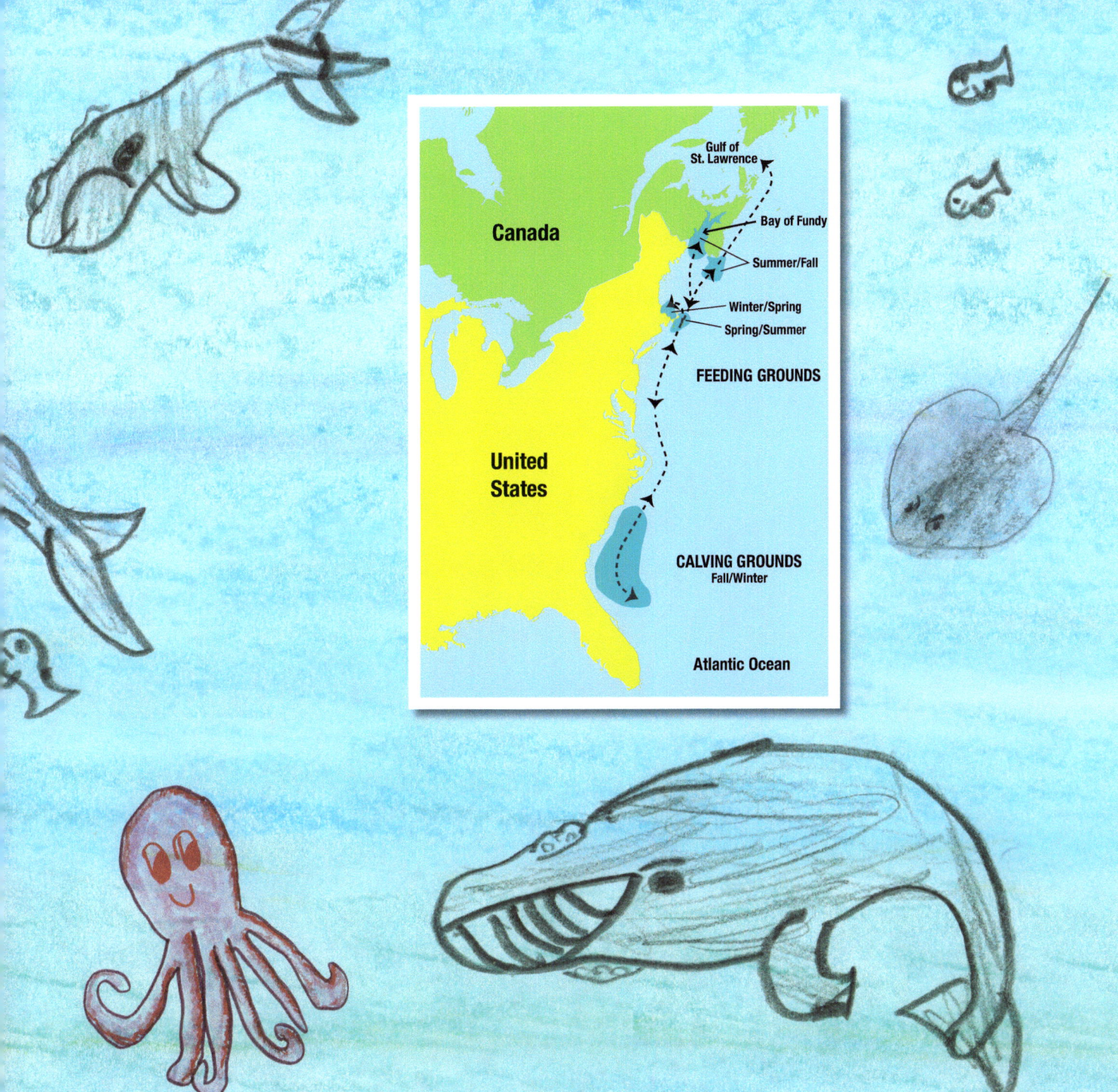

Gulf of
St. Lawrence

Canada

Bay of Fundy

Summer/Fall

Winter/Spring

Spring/Summer

FEEDING GROUNDS

United
States

CALVING GROUNDS
Fall/Winter

Atlantic Ocean

As we migrate, I see many other animals,
like squid, swordfish, and sharks.

When I breach I see the seagulls.
Jellyfish float in the tide.

I hear whales call in the distance.
I let out a whoop to greet them.

17

In Florida there are coral reefs with beautiful fish. Butterflyfish dart in and out of the coral. The light from the sun streams through the top layer of the water and shines off the coral, making something like a rainbow.

It's a beautiful place.

North Atlantic right whales are some of the most endangered animals in the world.

It started a long, long time ago, before I was born. Before electricity existed, whalers hunted us because they used our blubber to light oil lanterns, our bones for tools and decorative objects like sculptures, and our baleen for clothes, like corsets.

Humans named us right whales because we were the "right whales" to hunt. We are slow swimmers, so it was easy to catch us and kill us. And when we are dead we float, so the sailors could drag us to shore.

We were hunted so frequently that we almost became extinct.

For a long time, scientists thought we *were* extinct.

Although whaling has since been outlawed, that doesn't mean we are out of danger.

My species is close to extinction again.

Nowadays we're suffering because we get entangled in fishing ropes from lobster and crab traps. The ropes in our ocean are connected on one end to a trap, and on the other side to a buoy, so that fishers can find their traps when they are full.

When a whale gets entangled it is harder to swim. So the whale will burn more calories and will become really thin.

The ropes can also cut into our skin and blubber and give us terrible wounds. Some other whales I know who have gotten entangled had scars for the rest of their life. Baby whales who get entangled in ropes sometimes even drown.

There are also boats that can injure or kill
whales when they run into us by accident.

Ships produce a devastating noise. When we hear that noise, our ears hurt. Sometimes we can't find our family, because if we can't hear, we can't communicate.

Protecting calves is a hard job in our surroundings right now. As a mother, I should know.

Usually we would be producing more offspring than we have been. Last year we didn't have a lot of babies.

NOAA Permit #594-1759

Considering there are only about 400 North Atlantic right whales left, and only 100 are females, having more female children is very important to us. I, Kleenex, am a female, but I alone can't keep my species stable.

I'm generally happy to be a whale,
although I've gone through a lot of troubles.
This is where my story begins.

It was a normal day as I was swimming along, when suddenly I felt ropes pressing against my head and sides.

I twisted and turned, trying to get rid of the heavy fishing line. I thrashed and pulled, but that just made it worse. The rope was wrapped around my blowhole and stuck in my baleen.

I tried calling for help but no one came.
I was alone in the ocean.

Years later, the rope is still there.

It's been hard for me these past few years. After I got entangled, I got unhealthy and depressed.

NOAA Permit # 932-1905-MA-009526

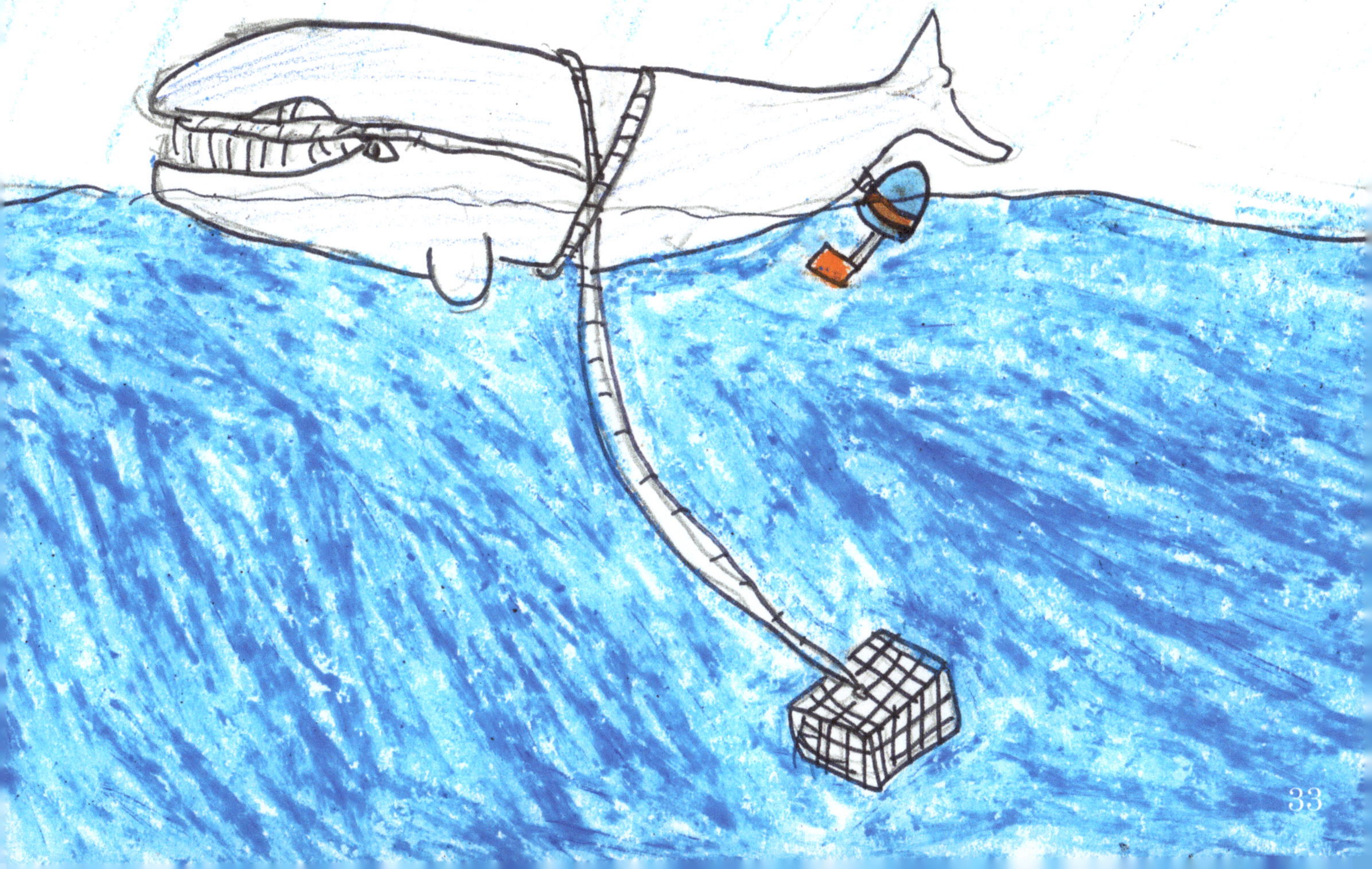

33

I try to swim, but the long rope is pulling on my back. The ropes are giving me grave pain all over. They rub against my skin. It feels like hot sandpaper.

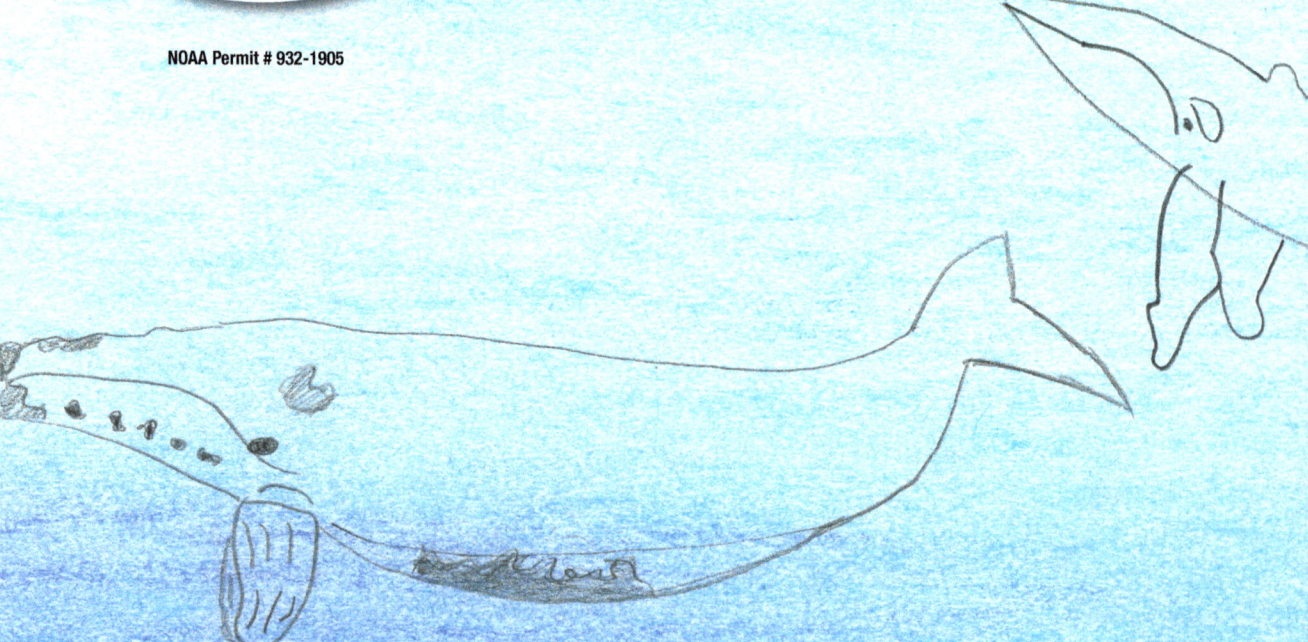

I've been more tired and I can't get enough food to eat. I have been getting skinnier, which may seem good to you humans, but it's not good for a whale.

Since I have less energy, I can't have any babies.
That means I'm not saving my species as much as
I'd like, which makes me sad. And with my age,
I might not have a chance for many more children.

I know a lot of other whales are suffering like me,
and worse.

And I can do nothing about it.

Several years after I got entangled in the uncomfortable ropes, I noticed a small boat that seemed to be following me.

NOAA Permit #932-1905

38

I immediately thought of the ropes, the great pain the humans have already given me. I didn't ever want to go near them again.

I swam away as fast as I could go. But the humans and the boat were always on my tail, literally and figuratively.

NOAA Permit # 932-1905

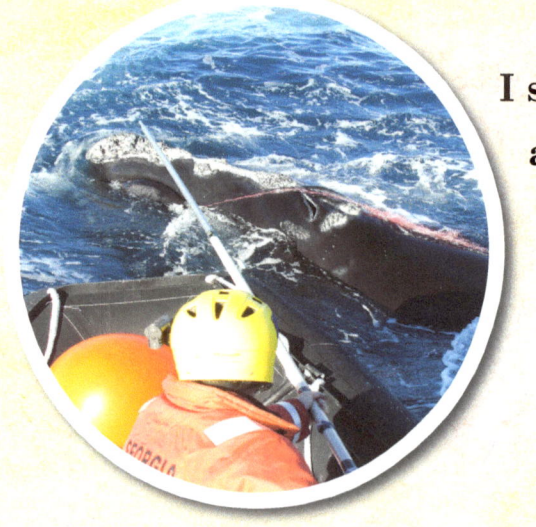

I saw them take out a bow and
arrow. They were going to shoot
me! I went underwater, the
only safe place I know.

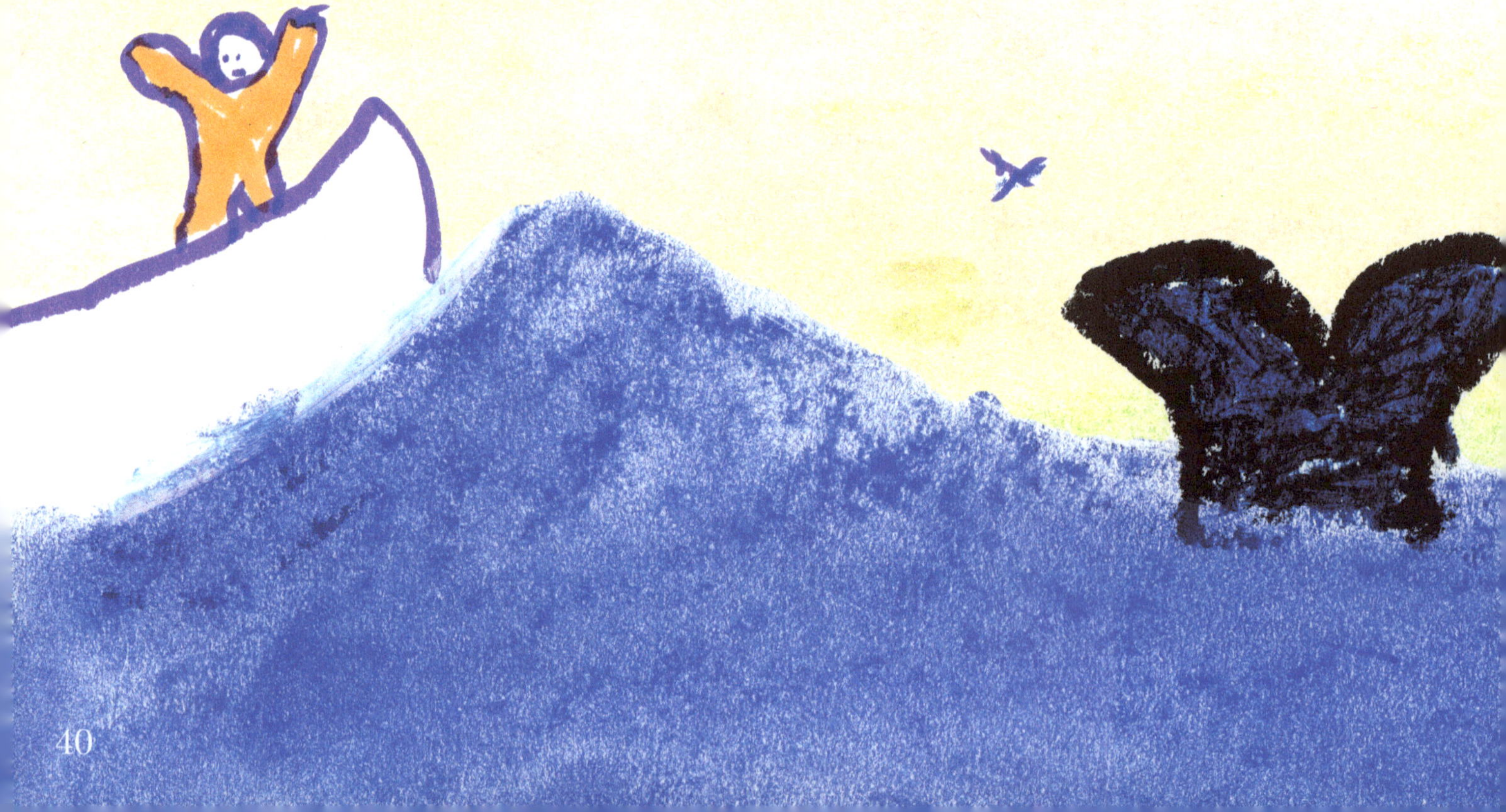

I felt a sharp pain near the back of my head, like a splinter. The arrow had hit and broken part of the line, so it had become frayed.

Then I realized: my rope was lighter. They were helping. The waves splashed over my blowhole as I twisted myself back to look. The shadow of the boat had gone.

I breached and splashed in the wondrous ocean.

42

Unfortunately, the dart only slightly
loosened the rope. But I hoped it
meant I would be free soon.

Even though whales are badly endangered, good things are happening too.

There are a lot of marine charities and nonprofit organizations working to protect us.

Scientists at the International Fund for Animal Welfare (IFAW) are working hard to increase our population.

Researchers are trying to promote ropeless fishing to prevent entanglements. Their idea is that when the fisher sends a signal to the trap, it pops up to the surface of the ocean.

Conservationists are also marking designated shipping lanes away from our favorite places in the ocean, to prevent boats from hitting us.

And they helped set up new rules to make sure that whales are safer from ships speeding by. Now all ships must slow down at certain times of the year to help prevent collisions.

One day I was swimming and I saw something amazing.
It almost brought tears to my eyes. I couldn't really
cry in the ocean, so I guess I was just really touched.
I saw ropeless fishing. I couldn't stop showing my
baleen plates. Or as humans say, smiling.

I have so many hopes for the future.

I hope that one day, humans will see that the ocean is for more than just their benefit. I want them to see that the ocean is a place where other animals live, and need to survive.

With so few right whales left, every whale matters.
In fact, if just a few more females survive each year,
our population can recover.

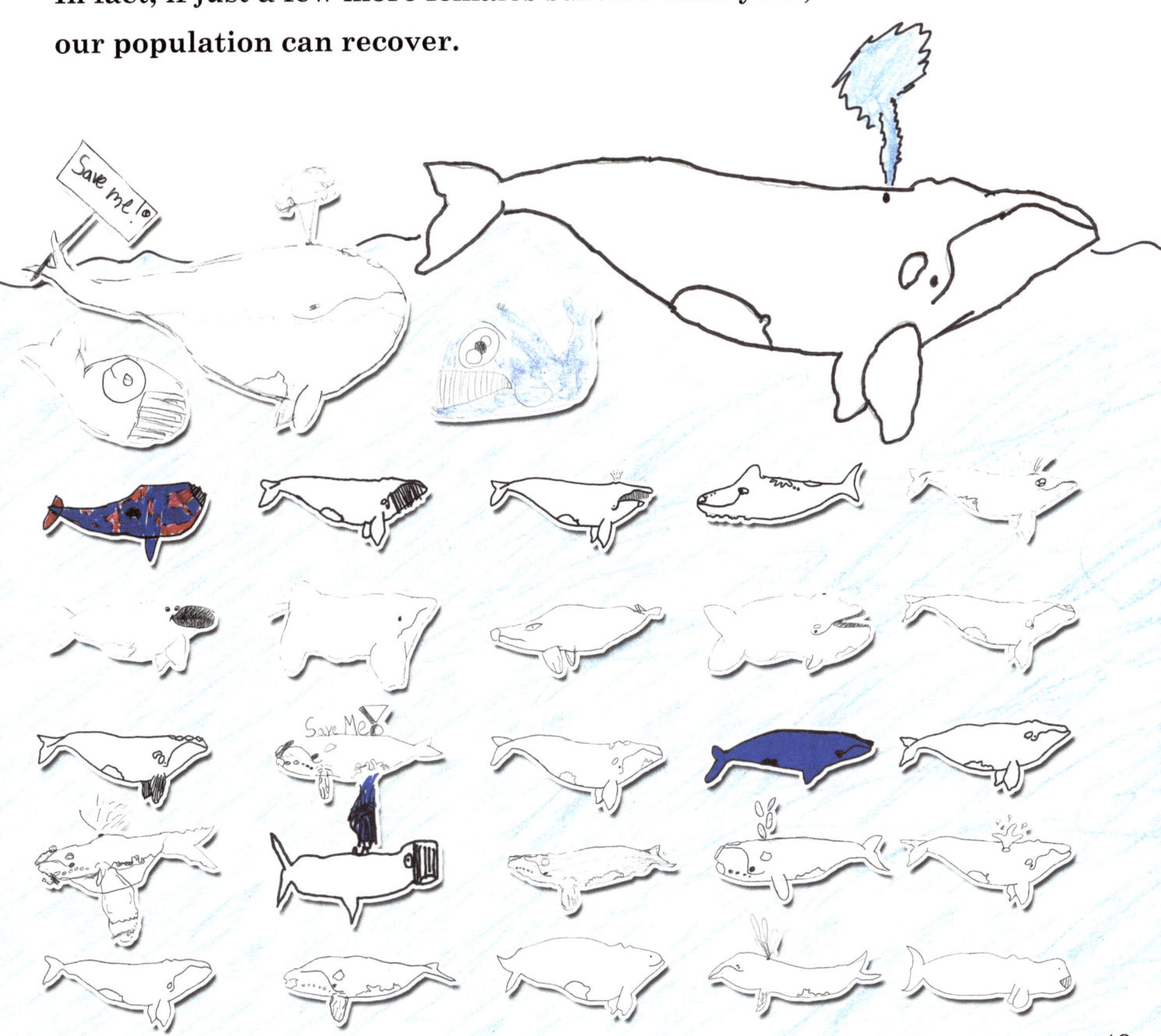

We have already spotted seven
calves this year. That's more than
last year, but not as many as we
would like. With just a bit more help
we can make more babies, and that
can increase our population.

I hope that more and more of us will be born
and grow to be amazing whales like me.

I hope some day all right whales will swim,
free of ropes, in our beautiful ocean home.

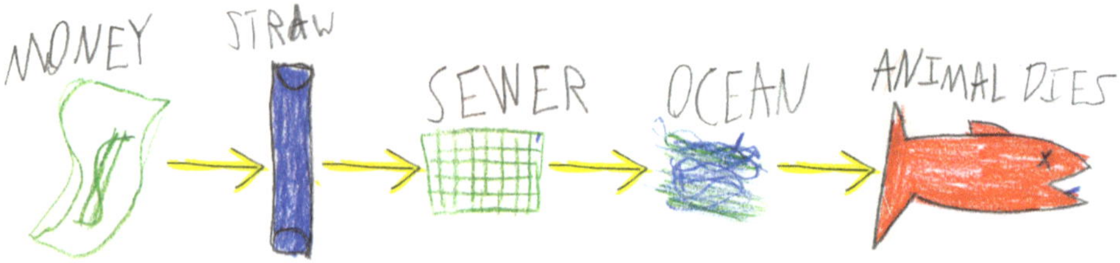

MONEY → STRAW → SEWER → OCEAN → ANIMAL DIES

It may seem like
there's no way that
we can be saved,
but we can.
There is still hope.

DON'T LITTER

What you can do to help me and my kind:

✓ Donate to organizations that help whales, like IFAW.

✓ If you buy seafood, look for labels that show it's certified wildlife friendly. By doing this you're buying food that wasn't caught using ropes which entangle us right whales.

✓ Don't buy bottled water, or any other plastic that can potentially enter our oceans.

✓ Talk to your elected representatives about stopping seismic testing, which damages our ears.

✓ If you see litter, pick it up and throw it away. Because if you don't it might end up in my ocean. And that can really harm not just us but a lot of other creatures.

Afterword

What would it take to convince a bunch of active fifth graders to forego recess twice or three times a week—even on the first warm days of spring? At our school—P.S. 107 in Brooklyn—students willingly gave up their cherished lunch and outdoor play periods, over the course of several months, to produce the book you hold in your hands. In a series of workshops, students researched and wrote the narrative, and created the stunning art for this heart-rending story—the tale of one North Atlantic right whale's struggle to navigate in an ocean forever changed by human industry.

One Special Whale is the sixth book in a series; in the past five years, our fifth graders have written about the plight of endangered Sumatran rhinos, African forest elephants, Bornean orangutans, Siberian tigers, and African grey parrots. These books are an annual project of Beast Relief, a PTA committee created to educate our students and school community about wildlife conservation—a project that complements the school's commitment to an ethic of care and stewardship of our fragile planet.

The collaborative project also nicely complements P.S. 107's social studies and English curriculum, especially its emphasis on developing strong writers. Our students work on both fiction and nonfiction writing projects—including memoir, informational and persuasive writing—beginning in kindergarten.

When the One Special books are published toward the end of the academic year, student authors and illustrators celebrate by inviting the younger grades to author readings. The younger students begin to look forward to becoming authors themselves in their final year at the school. At the readings, I always see the students' sense of pride in their work—and in their understanding that they have done something that, in some small way, has helped to save the whales—and elephants, and the rhinos, orangutans, tigers, and parrots. They leave P.S. 107 knowing that they have done something real and something important to make the world a better place.

Eve Litwack

Eve Litwack
Principal, P.S. 107 John W. Kimball Learning Center

Beast Relief, a PTA committee at P.S. 107 John W. Kimball Learning Center in Park Slope, Brooklyn, teaches children about the need for conservation, instills in them a love of animals and takes concrete steps to help animals far and near. Every year, in partnership with a wildlife organization, our fifth graders write and illustrate a book about a real endangered animal. All proceeds from the self-published books, which are available for purchase on Amazon.com, go directly to the wildlife organizations. *One Special Whale* is the sixth book in our One Special Animal series. Also available:

Acknowledgements

The Beast Relief Committee at P.S. 107 would like to thank the following people for their invaluable help and support.

The International Fund for Animal Welfare was a wonderful partner in the creation of this book. Kate Farinella, IFAW's Director of Global Communications, immediately embraced the project when we proposed it to her. Kate, along with Patrick Ramage, Director of Marine Conservation, and Hannah Myers, economic and policy advisor to IFAW's right whale campaign and guest investigator at the Woods Hole Oceanographic Institution, introduced us to Kleenex, fielded innumerable questions and provided crucial advice throughout the project. Hannah also traveled from Cape Cod to our school in Brooklyn and gave an inspiring presentation to the students about right whale conservation. She directed us to research articles and reviewed the text for errors.

Clay George, Senior Wildlife Biologist at the Georgia Department of Natural Resources, shared a cache of wonderful photographs with us for publication.

Maureen McLaughlin created the exquisite design for the book. Grace Sharfstein added her imaging touches to the book. Adrianna Dufay, Julia Austen-Brown, Linda Salzberg, Karin Ulman, and Tracy Tullis led the art and writing workshops. Jackie Cazar managed the details of publication. Katherine Eban provided guidance throughout.

The school's principal, Eve Litwack, and parent coordinator, Pamela Rosenberg, provided logistical and moral support for the project. P.S. 107's art teacher, Julie Brunner Cross, taught the students how to draw whales. Fifth grade teachers Michael Carlson, Shirley Hawkins, Ed Schulz, Katie Coombe, and Michele Dente offered technical support and put up with our mess in their classrooms.

And finally, enormous thanks to our fifth-grade authors and illustrators, who enthusiastically embraced the mission of helping to save the whales.

Text and illustrations copyright © 2019 by P.S. 107 John W. Kimball Learning Center

Photo credits: Cover and Page 4 and 28: Photos of Kleenex and 2009 calf by Wildlife Trust, taken with NOAA permit #594-1759; Pages 4, 9, 13 and 51: Photos of Kleenex courtesy of New England Aquarium; Page 15: Map © Shutterstock, adapted from E. Paul Oberlander, Woods Hole Oceanographic Institution Graphics; Data from North Atlantic Right Whale Consortium; Pages 13, 33, 34, 40, and 42: Photos of right whales courtesy of Florida Fish and Wildlife by Georgia Department of Natural Resources, NOAA permit #15488, 932-1905, and 932-1905-MA-009526; Page 14: Photo by Sea to Shore Alliance/NOAA, NOAA permit #15488; Page 31: Photo of Kleenex by Center for Coastal Studies, NOAA permit #18786; Page 38: Photo of right whale by EcoHealth Alliance, NOAA Permit #932-1905

Fifth Grade Authors and Illustrators

57

www.ingramcontent.com/pod-product-compliance
Lightning Source LLC
Chambersburg PA
CBHW060833290526
45792CB00006BB/1912